TURKEY
TOOTS

WRITTEN AND ILLUSTRATED BY
JANE BEXLEY

Tommy was a turkey with a knack for being silly.
His favorite way to have some fun was tooting willy-nilly.

His buddies laughed until they cried when gas would start to rise.
The girls would pinch their noses shut and sharply roll their eyes.

Tommy was a clever bird who'd never waste his skills,
he knew that all these awesome farts could bring him fame
and thrills!

Tomorrow was the festival with contests, games, and races. He planned to beat his friends by blasting fart bombs in their faces.

Before they started, grandpa turkey always took the stage,
to warn them of the things he learned when he was just their age.

"Go have some fun but also please be wary of the danger.
This time of year our farmer turns from friend to hungry stranger.
He's fixing a Thanksgiving feast and needs a tasty bird.
If you get caught, you'll be his meal. Remember what you've heard!"

"Okay, let's go now!" Tommy cried,
"let's get to all the fun!"
He lined up for the turkey trot then
burned some gas and won.

The turkey bowl was quite the sight with Tommy zooming by.
His farts propelled him down the field; he barely had to try!

The big sack race went quickly with his tooting shooting fine.
He turned his sack into a blimp and flew across the line.

He even won the pie contest, but not with speed and power.
He leaked some silent fumes that turned the other entries sour.

"Well that was sure a rotten day," he heard his friends complain.
"Why do we even try when Tommy's farts can rig the game?"

So that is what they thought about his awesome
farting feat?
He didn't need those grumpy friends that called his
farts a cheat.

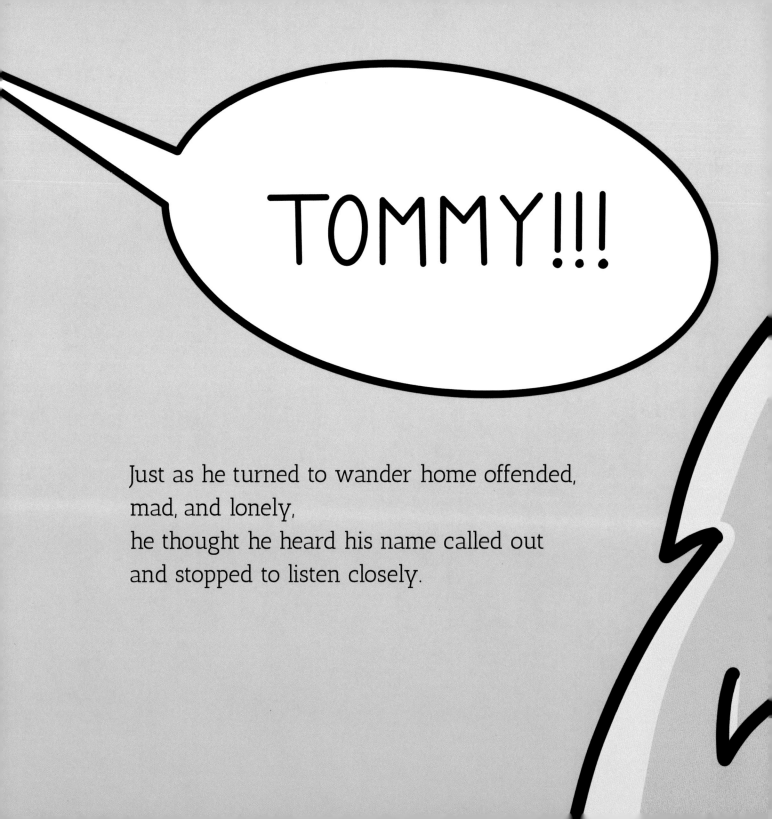

Just as he turned to wander home offended,
mad, and lonely,
he thought he heard his name called out
and stopped to listen closely.

"Tommy HELP!!!" his friends cried out. "He's got us, hurry please!"
"I'm coming!" Tommy hollered as he blew some booty breeze.

His friends were cornered in the barn with nowhere left
to go.
The farmer moved in closer, set to deal a fatal blow.

Tommy thought, "the pies I gassed smelled way too bad to eat,
maybe stinky birds will force the farmer to retreat!"

With all the power he could muster, Tommy let it fly.
He bombed the barn with toxic fumes and took off in the sky.
"Good grief what is that smell?" the farmer coughed and
grabbed his chest,
"I can't serve a stinky bird to all my dinner guests!"

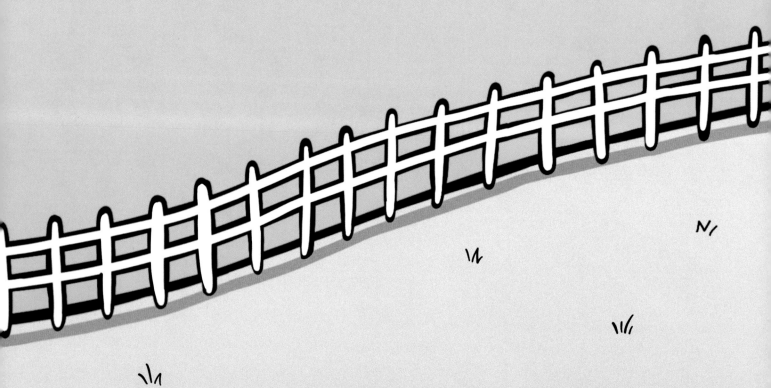

The turkeys cheered and thanked their friend for saving them from doom.
They'd never been so happy that his farts could clear a room!

"I'm sorry that I cheated," Tommy let out with a sigh.
"I'll just save my farts for when there's danger lurking by!"

And though they reeked of Tommy's toots
(much to the girls' dismay),
the turkeys danced in celebration that
Thanksgiving Day.

Made in United States
Orlando, FL
30 November 2024

54717190R00020